Beyond Anxiety's Grasp

Mastering Mindful Techniques, Cultivating Inner Peace,

and Embracing a Journey Toward Wellness

Karina Gibson

Table of Contents

INTRODUCTION

In my tenure as a psychiatrist, I've journeyed into the vast landscape of human emotion, confronting the pervasive shadow of anxiety. Each individual I've encountered has contributed a unique thread to the intricate tapestry of our collective understanding, revealing the profound and varied impact anxiety wields over lives. It's through these myriad encounters that "Beyond Anxiety's Grasp" was conceived—a testament to my deep-seated commitment to not only demystify anxiety as a clinical phenomenon but to address it as a fundamentally human experience. This book stands as a beacon of hope and a guide for those ensnared by anxiety's far-reaching tendrils, offering paths toward liberation.

Anxiety surpasses mere worry or stress, transcending the day-to-day challenges that transiently concern us. It represents a more insidious force, an undercurrent capable of undermining one's sense of safety and diminishing life's joys. Our journey through this book aims to delineate this distinction clearly, inviting readers to peer beneath the surface ripples to the depths where anxiety resides. In doing so, we will navigate the contours of anxiety—its symptoms, triggers, and both its physiological and psychological foundations. By illuminating anxiety's prevalence, affecting countless individuals globally, we strive to dismantle the solitude it engenders, reinforcing the notion that no one faces this struggle in isolation.

Designed as an exhaustive manual, "Beyond Anxiety's Grasp" weaves together the latest scientific research and rich anecdotal insights into a series of actionable, practical strategies. This book is your empowerment tool, imbuing you with the knowledge and techniques necessary to traverse the complexities of anxiety. You will discover how to pinpoint your anxiety triggers, understand the thought and behavior patterns that amplify your anxiety, and develop effective coping mechanisms and resilience strategies. This journey is transformative, guiding you from a place constrained by fear to a state of understanding, freedom, and peace.

The road to overcoming anxiety is fraught with complexities, characterized by both challenges and significant growth. From the outset, this book emphasizes the necessity of patience, perseverance, and, crucially, self-compassion. The process of battling anxiety is often marked by gradual progress and occasional setbacks. By setting realistic expectations and fostering a commitment to the healing process, this book pledges to be a constant source of support, offering understanding and encouragement every step of the way.

A pivotal yet often overlooked aspect of managing anxiety is the cultivation of self-compassion. The relentless critique from our internal voice can intensify anxiety's symptoms, entrenching us in a cycle of negativity. Advocating for a paradigm shift toward self-compassion, this book presents it as an indispensable element in the healing arsenal. Fostering a gentler, more understanding relationship with oneself can significantly ease the journey towards recovery. This book will explore strategies to nurture self-compassion, laying a foundation for a more tranquil and resilient existence.

To extract the maximum benefit from this book, an active, engaged approach is paramount. I encourage readers to immerse themselves fully in this journey—allocating dedicated time for reading and reflection, consistently applying the outlined practices, and maintaining a journal to document your thoughts and progression. Given the fluctuating nature of anxiety, some days will inevitably prove more challenging; it is during these times that the teachings of this book can provide profound solace and strength. Crafted to be a comforting companion through the highs and lows of your journey, this book illuminates the path forward during moments of obscurity.

"Beyond Anxiety's Grasp" is more than a guide; it is an invitation to embark on a transformative journey. It aspires to lead you step by step away from the shadow of anxiety towards a life of empowerment, unburdened by fear. This book is not solely about overcoming anxiety but about evolving—becoming more aware, compassionate, and resilient. As you turn each page, you're taking a significant step towards a future where anxiety no longer dictates your life's narrative.

In crafting this book, my aim is to extend a hand to those weighed down by anxiety, offering not just strategies for managing their condition but also a new lens through which to view their experiences. Anxiety, though daunting, can catalyze profound personal growth and strength. "Beyond Anxiety's Grasp" embodies this belief, affirming that profound transformation lies within each individual's reach. It is my honor to accompany you on this journey, providing insights and guidance distilled into a roadmap for healing and self-discovery.

This book is intended to bridge the gap between the personal and the universal, delivering insights and strategies rooted in scientific rigor yet accessible and applicable to everyday life. I hope that "Beyond Anxiety's Grasp" will serve as a source of comfort, guidance, and inspiration for those on the path to healing. I invite you to join me on this journey with an open heart and mind, ready to embrace the growth and transformation that lies ahead. Together, we will explore the depths of anxiety and emerge on the other side, not just free from fear but enriched by the journey. Welcome to the first step of your transformative journey toward a life beyond the grasp of anxiety.

CHAPTER 1

UNRAVELING ANXIETY

This chapter sets out to decode the mystery of anxiety, starting with recognizing its often misunderstood signs and symptoms. We'll uncover the science of how anxiety operates within the brain, differentiating it from fear, and identifying personal triggers. This chapter also highlights the profound impact lifestyle choices have on our mental health, offering practical advice for turning everyday decisions into powerful tools for anxiety management. Through understanding, we pave the way for empowerment and healing.

Recognizing Anxiety: Signs and Symptoms

Understanding anxiety in its full complexity requires a deep dive into the myriad ways it manifests across the physical, emotional, and cognitive landscapes of those it touches. This condition, often cloaked in ambiguity, reveals itself through a tapestry of symptoms that can fluctuate wildly from person to person, underscoring the highly individualized nature of anxiety experiences. Recognizing these signs and symptoms is pivotal, as it not only facilitates early intervention but also fosters empathy and understanding towards oneself and others grappling with anxiety.

Physical Symptoms: The Body's Alarm System

Anxiety triggers the body's primal fight-or-flight mechanism, designed as a survival instinct to respond to threats. However, when this response is activated in the absence of real danger, it can lead to an array of physical symptoms that are both distressing and debilitating. An increased heart rate is a common symptom, as the heart pumps more blood to prepare the body for perceived emergency actions. This heightened state can also cause palpitations, where the heart feels like it's pounding, fluttering, or beating irregularly, adding to the sensation of panic.

Sweating, trembling, and dizziness are additional manifestations of the body's heightened state of alert. These symptoms are often accompanied by an uncomfortable feeling of shortness of breath, which can escalate into hyperventilation as the individual tries to take in more oxygen in response to perceived danger. For some, these physical sensations culminate in panic attacks, acute episodes characterized by a sudden onslaught of fear or discomfort, accompanied by chest pain, a feeling of choking, or fear of dying.

Digestive disturbances frequently occur alongside anxiety, manifesting as nausea, stomach cramps, or diarrhea. The gastrointestinal system is particularly sensitive to stress and anxiety, leading to an upset stomach or changes in appetite. Muscle tension is another prevalent symptom, with individuals experiencing aches and pains, especially in the neck, shoulders, and back, as the body remains in a constant state of tension. Sleep disturbances further exacerbate physical discomfort, with difficulty falling asleep, staying asleep, or experiencing restorative sleep, leading to chronic fatigue and decreased physical resilience.

Emotional and Cognitive Symptoms: The Mind in Turmoil

Anxiety's impact extends beyond the physical, deeply affecting emotional and cognitive processes. Excessive worrying, characterized by persistent, exaggerated concerns about everyday matters, lies at the heart of anxiety's emotional turmoil. This worry is not limited to realistic concerns but extends to imagined scenarios, often spiraling into a cycle of fear and apprehension about future events.

Difficulty concentrating is a hallmark cognitive symptom of anxiety, with individuals finding themselves unable to focus or maintain attention, their minds preoccupied with anxious thoughts. This can severely impact productivity and the ability to perform tasks effectively, further fueling feelings of inadequacy or frustration. Anxiety can also manifest as irritability or a short fuse, with minor irritations provoking disproportionate responses.

A pervasive sense of dread or impending doom is a distressing emotional symptom, leaving individuals in a constant state of fear about what the future may hold. This sense of foreboding can be paralyzing, affecting decision-making and daily activities. Avoidance behavior is another common response, where individuals steer clear of situations or activities that they fear might trigger their anxiety, further limiting their life experiences and potential for enjoyment.

Variability Across Anxiety Disorders: A Spectrum of Experiences

The experience of anxiety is not uniform, varying significantly across different anxiety disorders, each characterized by its distinct patterns of symptoms. Generalized Anxiety Disorder (GAD) is typified by chronic, exaggerated worrying about multiple aspects of life, whereas Panic Disorder involves recurrent, unexpected panic attacks. Phobias center around intense fear or aversion to specific objects or situations, such as heights, flying, or certain animals.

Social Anxiety Disorder is characterized by an intense fear of social situations due to worries about being judged or embarrassed. Obsessive-Compulsive Disorder (OCD) involves repetitive, unwanted thoughts (obsessions) and behaviors (compulsions) that the individual feels driven to perform. Post-Traumatic Stress Disorder (PTSD) results from experiencing or witnessing a traumatic event, leading to persistent re-experiencing of the trauma, avoidance of trauma-related cues, and heightened arousal.

Understanding the signs and symptoms of anxiety, in all its forms and manifestations, is crucial for those seeking to navigate the complexities of this condition. It empowers individuals with the knowledge to seek help, fosters a compassionate self-awareness, and paves the way for effective management strategies. As we delve further into anxiety's labyrinth, the importance of recognizing these symptoms becomes ever clearer, offering a beacon of hope for those seeking to understand and ultimately transcend their anxiety.

The Science Behind Anxiety: Understanding Your Brain

Anxiety, often perceived as a purely psychological condition, is deeply rooted in complex neurological and biochemical processes. Understanding the science behind anxiety not only demystifies the condition but also empowers individuals with the knowledge that their experiences have a tangible physiological basis. The human brain, a marvel of evolution, plays a pivotal role in the experience of anxiety, with specific structures and neurotransmitters orchestrating a symphony of reactions that constitute the anxious response.

Neurological Structures Involved in Anxiety

At the heart of the brain's involvement in anxiety is the amygdala, an almond-shaped set of neurons located deep within the brain's medial temporal lobe. Known as the brain's "fear center," the amygdala plays a crucial role in processing emotions, particularly fear and anxiety. When an individual perceives a threat, real or imagined, the amygdala is activated, initiating a cascade of physiological responses designed to prepare the body for a fight-or-flight response. This response, while essential for survival in dangerous situations, can become maladaptive in the absence of actual danger, leading to the persistent state of heightened alertness characteristic of anxiety disorders.

The prefrontal cortex, the brain's center for higher-order cognitive functions, including decision-making, impulse control, and social behavior, also plays a significant role in anxiety. It's responsible for modulating the response of the amygdala, assessing the threat level, and determining an appropriate reaction. In individuals with anxiety, the prefrontal cortex may not effectively regulate the amygdala's response, leading to an exaggerated fear reaction to non-threatening stimuli.

The hippocampus, another crucial brain structure, is involved in forming and retrieving memories, including those associated with fear. Its role in anxiety involves linking specific environmental or contextual cues with fear responses, which can contribute to the development of phobias and post-traumatic stress disorder (PTSD).

The Role of Neurotransmitters in Anxiety

Neurotransmitters, the brain's chemical messengers, play a vital role in regulating mood and emotions, including anxiety. Serotonin and gamma-aminobutyric acid (GABA) are two neurotransmitters known for their calming effects on the brain. Low levels of serotonin are associated with increased anxiety, depression, and other mood disorders, suggesting its critical role in maintaining emotional balance. GABA, the primary inhibitory neurotransmitter in the brain, counteracts the excitatory signals in the central nervous system, promoting relaxation and reducing anxiety. Medications that enhance GABA activity are often used in treating anxiety disorders.

Conversely, neurotransmitters like adrenaline (epinephrine) and cortisol, the stress hormone, facilitate the body's fight-or-flight response. Adrenaline stimulates an increase in heart rate, raises blood pressure, and enhances the body's energy levels, readying it for rapid response. Cortisol, released by the adrenal glands in response to stress, can provide a quick burst of energy and immunity, sharpen memory, and increase pain tolerance. However, chronic activation of this stress response system, with prolonged cortisol and adrenaline release, can lead to persistent anxiety and contribute to the development of anxiety disorders.

Understanding Anxiety's Physiological Basis

Grasping the neurological and biochemical underpinnings of anxiety provides a clearer picture of why anxiety feels so overwhelming and why it's not easily controlled by sheer willpower. This understanding fosters compassion for oneself and others dealing with anxiety, emphasizing that anxiety disorders are not a result of personal failure or weakness but rather the consequence of complex biological processes.

Moreover, understanding the science behind anxiety can guide more effective treatment strategies, from pharmacological interventions targeting neurotransmitter imbalances to psychotherapeutic approaches aimed at altering brain activity and responses. Cognitive-behavioral therapy (CBT), for instance, can help retrain the brain to respond differently to anxiety-provoking situations, effectively altering the neural pathways involved in the anxiety response.

In summary, anxiety is a multifaceted condition with deep roots in the brain's structure and chemistry. By unraveling the science behind anxiety, individuals can gain insights into their experiences, reducing stigma and paving the way for more informed and compassionate approaches to managing this condition. This knowledge not only empowers individuals with a sense of control over their anxiety but also highlights the importance of seeking professional help in addressing the physiological aspects of anxiety disorders.

Common Triggers and How to Identify Yours

Understanding and identifying your anxiety triggers is akin to embarking on a deep-sea expedition where the waters are both mysterious and revealing. Each dive brings you closer to understanding the nuances of your emotional undercurrents, offering insights that are pivotal for navigating the tumultuous waves of anxiety. This comprehensive journey requires not just a map but a detailed guide that encompasses the breadth of common triggers while emphasizing the highly individual nature of anxiety. It's a voyage of discovery, self-awareness, and ultimately, empowerment.

Common Triggers of Anxiety

- **Social Situations**: The labyrinth of social interactions is fraught with potential triggers. From the fear of public speaking, which taps into deep-seated fears of exposure and judgment, to the nuances of navigating interpersonal dynamics at gatherings, social anxiety encompasses a broad spectrum. This form of anxiety often stems from a core fear of rejection or inadequacy, magnified in settings where one feels vulnerable to the scrutiny of others.

- **Health Concerns**: In an age where information is at our fingertips, health-related anxiety has burgeoned, often fueled by incessant online searches that lead down rabbit holes of worst-case scenarios. This trigger is characterized not just by a fear of illness but by an overarching dread of mortality and the unknown, making every ache a harbinger of doom and every doctor's visit a trial.

- **Financial Issues**: Economic instability stands as a monolith of anxiety, casting long shadows over one's sense of security and autonomy. The ripple effects of financial stress can touch every aspect of life, from basic survival needs to social status and self-esteem. This form of anxiety is insidious, often creeping into thoughts unbidden, turning planning and foresight into worry and dread.

- **Significant Life Changes**: The human psyche craves stability and any deviation from the known—be it through relocation, career changes, or shifts in personal relationships—can trigger significant anxiety. These milestones, while part of the human experience, challenge our adaptability and resilience, often stirring fears about our ability to cope and succeed in new environments.

- **Past Trauma**: Trauma imprints itself deeply within the psyche, with certain stimuli acting as keys that unlock these dormant fears, triggering profound anxiety or panic. The challenge lies in the unpredictable nature of these triggers, as they can be activated by seemingly unrelated events or sensations, linking the present inexorably to the past.

Identifying Your Triggers

The process of uncovering your unique anxiety triggers is both an art and a science, demanding introspection, observation, and a willingness to confront uncomfortable truths.

- **Journaling with Insight**: Transform your journal into a tool of discovery. Beyond mere events, delve into the fabric of your experiences—your thoughts, bodily sensations, emotional responses—before, during, and after moments of heightened anxiety. This detailed log serves as a mirror, reflecting patterns and triggers that might otherwise remain obscured.

- **Exploring Your Narrative**: Your life story holds keys to understanding your anxiety triggers. Reflect on your history, relationships, and significant events. Identifying recurring themes in your anxious responses can illuminate underlying triggers, offering a narrative thread that weaves through your experiences.

- **Embracing Mindfulness**: Mindfulness practice hones your attention, sharpening your focus on the present moment. This heightened awareness becomes a beacon, guiding you to recognize the onset of anxiety and its triggers as they emerge, fostering a mindful response rather than a reactive one.

- **Leveraging External Perspectives**: Engage in dialogue with trusted individuals or a therapist who can offer external perspectives on your anxiety patterns. This collaborative exploration can uncover triggers you might have minimized or overlooked, providing a broader view of your anxiety landscape.

- **Guided Exposure and Reflection**: With professional guidance, cautiously approach situations you suspect might be triggers. This methodical exposure, coupled with reflection and support, can demystify your triggers, reducing their power over your emotional state.

Armed with knowledge of your triggers, the focus shifts from identification to mastery. Understanding your triggers allows for the tailoring of coping strategies that resonate with your experience. This might include specific relaxation techniques for immediate relief, cognitive-behavioral strategies for long-term management, or therapeutic interventions for deeper issues.

Identifying your anxiety triggers is not about charting a course away from anxiety altogether but learning to navigate its waters with skill and confidence. It's about transforming your relationship with anxiety, from one of avoidance and fear to one of understanding and resilience. This detailed exploration of your triggers, coupled with targeted coping strategies, opens the door to a life where anxiety, while present, no longer controls your journey.

Anxiety vs. Fear: Distinguishing Between the Two

The exploration of human emotions reveals a complex web where fear and anxiety, two of the most primal responses, play critical roles. Though often used interchangeably in casual conversation, fear and anxiety differ significantly, not only in their triggers and manifestations but also in how they influence behavior and mental processing. Distinguishing between these two emotional states is not an exercise in semantics; rather, it's an endeavor to understand the underpinnings of our reactions to the world around us, offering a clearer path to effective coping and management strategies.

The Anatomy of Fear

Fear is an immediate, intense emotional response to a real, identifiable threat or danger. It's a survival mechanism deeply embedded in the human psyche, serving an evolutionary purpose by preparing the body to react swiftly to immediate threats. This reaction, known as the fight-or-flight response, is a testament to fear's direct link to physical survival. For example, encountering a wild animal triggers a fear response that mobilizes the body for quick, decisive action—either to confront the threat or to flee from it.

The neurological response to fear is primarily orchestrated by the amygdala, a small, almond-shaped structure in the brain that processes emotions. Upon perceiving a threat, the amygdala sends distress signals to other parts of the brain, including the hypothalamus, initiating a cascade of physiological reactions. These include the release of adrenaline and cortisol, which result in increased heart rate, heightened alertness, and a surge of energy—all aimed at enhancing the body's capacity for a rapid response to danger.

The Complexity of Anxiety

Anxiety, while related to fear, is distinct in its anticipatory nature. It is a diffuse, often persistent concern or worry about potential threats or negative outcomes that are not immediately present or, in some cases, may not be clearly defined at all. Anxiety encompasses a range of experiences, from generalized worry about everyday matters to specific anxieties triggered by particular situations (such as social settings or flying) and conditions like panic disorder, where the anxiety becomes so intense it leads to panic attacks.

Unlike fear, which is typically short-lived and tied to a clear and present danger, anxiety can linger, coloring one's outlook and interactions with a constant sense of apprehension or dread. It involves not just an emotional response but a cognitive one, where the mind becomes preoccupied with potential threats, often overestimating their likelihood or severity and underestimating one's ability to cope with them.

This anticipatory aspect of anxiety is primarily managed by the prefrontal cortex, the brain's center for higher-order thinking and planning. The prefrontal cortex evaluates potential future scenarios, including their possible threats and outcomes. However, in states of anxiety, this evaluation process can become skewed, leading to a heightened state of worry about events that may never occur.

Moreover, anxiety's persistence can also be attributed to the hippocampus, another critical brain structure involved in forming and retrieving memories. The hippocampus links environmental or situational cues to emotional responses, which can exacerbate anxiety when certain cues are perceived to signal potential threats based on past experiences.

Interplay and Distinction

Understanding the distinction between fear and anxiety is foundational to navigating the complexities of human emotions and implementing effective coping strategies. Fear's direct, immediate response to threat has clear survival benefits, necessitating rapid, often physical, reactions. In contrast, anxiety's diffuse, anticipatory nature calls for different management strategies, often involving cognitive behavioral techniques aimed at addressing the underlying patterns of thought that fuel worry and apprehension.

Moreover, the differentiation between fear and anxiety highlights the importance of addressing these emotions' physiological and psychological dimensions. While fear may require immediate physical safety measures, anxiety often demands a more nuanced approach, including mindfulness practices, stress reduction techniques, and, in some cases, therapeutic intervention to untangle the cognitive processes at play.

In conclusion, fear and anxiety, though intertwined, serve different functions and present unique challenges. A deeper understanding of these emotional states, their triggers, and their manifestations allows for a more informed and effective approach to managing them. Recognizing whether one is experiencing fear in response to an immediate threat or anxiety over anticipated events can empower individuals to apply the most appropriate coping mechanisms, paving the way for healthier psychological and emotional well-being.

The Role of Lifestyle in Anxiety Management

The intricate dance between lifestyle and anxiety is one of profound complexity and undeniable impact. Modern research continues to uncover the extent to which daily habits and choices can influence, mitigate, or exacerbate anxiety levels. While lifestyle changes alone may not serve as a panacea for anxiety disorders, their role in managing and potentially reducing anxiety symptoms is significant. This comprehensive exploration delves into the various lifestyle factors such as diet, exercise, sleep, and time management, offering evidence-based recommendations for creating a life that supports mental health and well-being.

Diet and Anxiety

The adage "you are what you eat" holds a kernel of truth, especially when examining the relationship between diet and anxiety. Nutritional psychiatry, an emerging field, underscores the link between food intake and mental health. A balanced diet, rich in whole foods, provides the essential nutrients needed for optimal brain function and can influence mood and anxiety levels. Omega-3 fatty acids, found in fish such as salmon and in flaxseeds, have been shown to reduce symptoms of anxiety. These essential fats play a crucial role in brain health, contributing to the fluidity of cell membranes and supporting neurotransmitter function.

Conversely, diets high in refined sugars and caffeine can exacerbate anxiety symptoms. Sugar can lead to spikes and crashes in blood sugar levels, which may increase feelings of anxiety and irritability. Caffeine, a stimulant, can mimic the physical sensations of anxiety—increasing heart rate and tension, thus potentially heightening anxiety in sensitive individuals. Moderating these substances and focusing on a diet rich in vegetables, fruits, lean proteins, and whole grains can contribute to a more stable mood and decreased anxiety levels.

Exercise as a Counter to Anxiety

Physical activity is a powerful tool in the arsenal against anxiety. Regular exercise has been consistently shown to have a profound impact on mental health, thanks to its ability to release endorphins, the body's natural painkillers, and mood elevators. Exercise also helps regulate the body's stress hormones, such as adrenaline and cortisol, in the long term. Aerobic exercises, such as jogging, swimming, cycling, and walking, have been particularly noted for their anxiety-reducing effects. The key is consistency and finding a form of exercise that is enjoyable and sustainable, integrating it as a regular part of one's lifestyle.

The Restorative Power of Sleep

Sleep and anxiety exist in a bidirectional relationship, where anxiety can lead to sleep disturbances, and poor sleep can exacerbate anxiety. Ensuring adequate, restful sleep is paramount in managing anxiety levels. Practices that promote good sleep hygiene, such as establishing a regular sleep schedule, creating a restful environment free from screens and disturbances, and engaging in relaxing activities before bed, can enhance sleep quality. Additionally, mindfulness and relaxation techniques can help quiet the mind and reduce the sleep disruptions often caused by anxiety.

Mastering Time Management

Poor time management can lead to stress and anxiety, with procrastination and the resultant crunch times serving as significant triggers. Developing effective time management skills, such as prioritizing tasks, breaking down larger projects into manageable steps, and setting realistic deadlines, can reduce the overwhelm and anxiety associated with a heavy workload or busy lifestyle. Tools and techniques such as the Eisenhower Box or the Pomodoro Technique can aid in organizing tasks and managing time more efficiently, thereby reducing anxiety.

Integrating Stress Management Techniques

Incorporating stress management techniques into daily life is essential for reducing anxiety. Practices such as mindfulness meditation, deep breathing exercises, yoga, and progressive muscle relaxation can help lower stress levels and promote a state of calm. These practices not only provide immediate relief from the physical sensations of anxiety but, over time, can also retrain the brain to respond more calmly to stressors.

In summary, while lifestyle modifications alone may not eliminate anxiety disorders, they play a crucial role in managing anxiety levels and improving overall well-being. By adopting a balanced diet, engaging in regular physical activity, ensuring restful sleep, mastering time management, and incorporating stress reduction techniques, individuals can create a supportive foundation for mental health, paving the way towards reduced anxiety and enhanced quality of life.

CHAPTER 2

TOOLS FOR TACKLING ANXIETY

This chapter is a gateway to mastering anxiety, introducing a suite of empowering strategies. It begins with the art of breathing techniques for instant calm, guiding you into the peaceful realms of mindfulness and meditation. You'll learn cognitive behavioral techniques to rewire persistent negative thoughts and discover how physical activity acts as a natural anxiety antidote. The narrative also navigates the crucial role of diet in mental well-being, distinguishing nourishing choices from those that exacerbate anxiety. Embark on this journey to reclaim peace and control.

Breathing Techniques for Immediate Relief

The utilization of breathing techniques as a means to alleviate anxiety symptoms is both an art and a science, deeply embedded in centuries of practice yet firmly supported by contemporary scientific understanding. These techniques stand as powerful tools in the immediate reduction of anxiety, primarily through their direct influence on the body's autonomic nervous system. Conscious regulation of breathing serves as a link between the conscious and unconscious aspects of the mind, enabling people to directly stimulate the parasympathetic nervous system, also known as the "rest and digest" system. This helps in reducing the body's reaction to stress.

Physiological Underpinnings

When confronted with stress or perceived threats, the body's sympathetic nervous system is activated, preparing the individual for "fight or flight" through increased heart rate, rapid breathing, and heightened alertness. However, this state can be counterbalanced by activating the parasympathetic nervous system through deep, controlled breathing exercises. This shift promotes a decrease in heart rate, a lowering of blood pressure, and a reduction in stress hormone levels, thereby inducing a state of calm and relaxation.

The activation of the parasympathetic nervous system through breathing is mediated by the vagus nerve, one of the longest nerves in the body, which plays a crucial role in heart rate, digestion, and overall mood regulation. By engaging in specific breathing practices, we can stimulate the vagus nerve, encouraging a parasympathetic response that counteracts the stress-induced activations of the sympathetic nervous system.

Exploration of Breathing Techniques

Diaphragmatic Breathing

Diaphragmatic breathing, also known as abdominal or belly breathing, emphasizes full engagement of the diaphragm, promoting more efficient and deeper breaths. This method not only improves oxygen exchange but also stimulates the parasympathetic nervous system, facilitating a relaxation response.

1. **Setup**: Choose a quiet, comfortable place to sit or lie down. Ease your shoulders down and position one hand on your chest while placing the other hand on your stomach.

2. **Breathing In**: Slowly inhale through your nose, focusing on drawing the breath down toward your abdomen. The hand on your stomach should move upwards, while the hand on your chest should stay mostly stationary.

3. **Holding the Breath**: After inhaling deeply, hold your breath momentarily. This pause allows for maximum oxygen absorption.

4. **Breathing Out**: Breathe out slowly and completely, using either your mouth or nose based on what feels best for you, noticing the hand on your stomach descend as your diaphragm eases.

5. **Repetition**: Continue this pattern for several minutes, gradually increasing the duration as comfort with the technique grows.

The 4-7-8 Technique

The 4-7-8 breathing method, created by Dr. Andrew Weil, draws its inspiration from pranayama, an age-old yoga breathing practice. It is designed to bring the body into a state of deep relaxation and has been advocated as a method for reducing anxiety and promoting sleep.

1. **Positioning**: Sit with your back straight Rest the tip of your tongue against the upper part of your mouth, right behind your front teeth, and maintain this position for the duration of the exercise.

2. **Exhalation**: Begin by completely exhaling through your mouth, making a whoosh sound.

3. **Inhalation**: Seal your lips and quietly draw air in through your nose, counting to four in your mind.

4. **Hold**: Hold your breath for a count of seven.

5. **Exhalation**: Open your mouth and exhale completely, making a whoosh sound to a count of eight.

6. **Cycle**: This completes one cycle.

7. Perform the sequence three additional times, achieving a total of four breathing cycles.

Box Breathing

Box breathing, also known as square breathing, is a simple yet effective technique used by athletes, military personnel, and others to gain control over their physiological and psychological state.

1. **Preparation**: Sit or stand in a comfortable position, ensuring your posture supports easy breathing.

2. **Inhalation**: Begin by slowly exhaling all of the air out of your lungs. Then, inhale through your nose for a count of four, deeply filling your lungs.

3. **Holding the Breath**: Hold your breath at the top of the inhalation for a count of four.

4. **Exhalation**: Slowly exhale through your mouth for a count of four, emptying your lungs.

5. **Pause**: After exhaling, hold your breath for another count of four before starting the next inhalation.

6. **Continuation**: Repeat this pattern for several minutes, focusing on maintaining even and steady counts.

By integrating these breathing techniques into daily practice, individuals can gain immediate tools for addressing the onset of anxiety symptoms. These practices not only offer short-term relief but also contribute to long-term well-being by enhancing the body's capacity to return to a state of calm and balance in the face of stressors.

Mindfulness and Meditation: Cultivating Peace

The practices of mindfulness and meditation stand as beacons of tranquility in the tumultuous sea of modern life, offering not just a refuge from the storm of anxiety but a profound method to transform one's engagement with the world. Rooted in ancient wisdom and validated by contemporary psychological research, these practices invite us to anchor ourselves in the richness of the present moment, cultivating a landscape of internal peace that endures beyond fleeting external circumstances.

The Essence of Mindfulness

Mindfulness is the intentional cultivation of a nonjudgmental, moment-to-moment awareness. It's an invitation to awaken to the experiences of our lives, to step out of the automatic pilot mode driven by habit and distraction, and to step into a richer, more direct experience of the present. By practicing mindfulness, we learn to observe our thoughts, feelings, bodily sensations, and the environment around us with a gentle, open curiosity. This observation without judgment allows us to recognize that thoughts and emotions are transient by nature, reducing their power to dominate our internal landscape.

Meditation: A Pathway to Inner Peace

Meditation, often used as a practice to cultivate mindfulness, involves specific techniques designed to focus the mind, regulate the breath, and promote emotional equilibrium. Various forms of meditation cater to different needs and preferences, yet all share the common goal of fostering a state of calm awareness.

- **Guided Imagery Meditation**: This technique utilizes the power of the imagination to evoke calming, peaceful images within the mind's eye. Participants might be guided to envision themselves in a serene natural setting or to imagine a healing light enveloping them. By focusing on these positive, tranquil images, the mind is drawn away from anxiety-producing thoughts, facilitating a state of relaxation.

- **Loving-Kindness Meditation (Metta)**: This practice involves directing feelings of love, compassion, and goodwill first toward oneself and then, in widening circles, toward others. This form of meditation can dismantle barriers of fear and isolation, replacing them with a sense of interconnectedness and goodwill. It is particularly effective in mitigating the self-critical and isolating aspects of anxiety, fostering a sense of belonging and self-acceptance.

- **Body Scan Meditation**: Through progressively focusing attention on different parts of the body, practitioners are encouraged to become aware of physical sensations without attempting to change them. This heightened awareness can reveal areas of tension and stress, and the practice of nonjudgmental observation can lead to a spontaneous release of this tension, promoting physical relaxation and mental clarity.

Incorporating Mindfulness and Meditation into Daily Life

The true power of mindfulness and meditation lies in their application beyond the meditation cushion—infusing daily activities with presence and intention.

- **Regular Practice**: Establishing a consistent meditation practice, even if for just a few minutes each day, can lay a strong foundation for mindfulness. As this practice matures over time, its positive effects spread across different areas of life.

- **Mindfulness in Routine Activities**: Choosing routine tasks as opportunities for mindfulness practice—whether it's mindful eating, walking, or even showering—allows for the cultivation of presence throughout the day. This approach transforms mundane activities into rituals of awareness, enriching everyday life with depth and meaning.

- **Breath as an Anchor**: Returning to the breath serves as a powerful tool for centering oneself in moments of stress or overwhelm. This simple yet profound act of focusing on the breath can serve as an immediate conduit to the present moment, dissolving anxiety's grip.

- **Utilizing Digital Resources**: The abundance of digital resources, including mindfulness apps, online courses, and guided meditations, provides accessible pathways for deepening one's practice. These resources can offer guidance, structure, and community support for those on the journey of cultivating mindfulness and meditation.

Embracing mindfulness and meditation invites a radical shift in how we relate to our internal and external worlds. It's a journey from reactivity to response, from distraction to presence, and from anxiety to peace. By dedicating ourselves to these practices, we open the door to a life characterized by deeper engagement, resilience, and a profound sense of well-being that transcends the ebbs and flows of life's uncertainties.

Cognitive Behavioral Techniques: Reshaping Thoughts

Cognitive Behavioral Therapy (CBT) is an extensively researched and empirically supported treatment methodology for anxiety disorders, rooted in the interconnectivity of thoughts, emotions, and behaviors. It posits that negative and distorted thought patterns contribute significantly to the anxiety experience, affecting an individual's emotional state and actions. By identifying, challenging, and altering these maladaptive thought processes, CBT aims to alleviate anxiety symptoms and foster healthier cognitive patterns.

Foundations of CBT

CBT is predicated on the cognitive model of emotional response, which suggests that our thoughts about a situation affect how we feel and behave, not the situation itself. This model implies that even when an external situation cannot be changed, modifying one's perception of it can reduce anxiety and improve functional outcomes. The structured nature of CBT, typically delivered in a series of time-limited, goal-oriented sessions, focuses on specific problems, making it a practical approach to mental health treatment.

Cognitive Restructuring: Reframing the Mind

One of the central techniques in CBT is cognitive restructuring, a process aimed at identifying and challenging irrational or maladaptive thoughts. Cognitive restructuring involves several steps:

1. **Identification of Automatic Thoughts**: The initial phase involves training individuals to become acutely aware of their automatic thoughts—the spontaneous, often critical, thoughts that arise in response to stimuli. This awareness is crucial for pinpointing the thoughts that contribute to anxiety.

2. **Evaluation of Thoughts**: This step encourages individuals to examine their automatic thoughts critically, assessing their accuracy and helpfulness. Techniques such as the "evidence for and against" method are used to objectively evaluate the reality of these thoughts.

3. **Identification and Challenge of Cognitive Distortions**: CBT therapists guide individuals in recognizing specific cognitive distortions that warp their thinking. This might involve exercises that highlight tendencies towards black-and-white thinking, catastrophizing, or overgeneralization.

4. **Development of New Perspectives**: Individuals learn to replace identified distortions with more accurate and balanced thoughts. This process often involves perspective-taking, considering the best and worst outcomes, and finding the middle ground.

Exposure Therapy: Facing Fears Directly

Exposure therapy is a cornerstone of CBT for specific anxiety disorders such as phobias and PTSD. This approach involves:

- **Graded Exposure**: Starting with less anxiety-inducing situations and gradually moving to more feared scenarios, this method helps individuals slowly build tolerance to their fears.

- **Systematic Desensitization**: Often combined with relaxation techniques, this strategy involves exposing individuals to their fears while in a relaxed state, diminishing the usual anxiety response over time.

- **Prolonged Exposure**: Used primarily for PTSD, this involves repeated, prolonged exposure to trauma-related stimuli without the expected adverse outcomes, helping to extinguish the fear response.

Coping Strategies Beyond the Basics

CBT arms individuals with a variety of coping strategies tailored to confront and manage anxiety effectively:

- **Mindfulness Techniques**: Beyond relaxation, mindfulness techniques encourage a non-judgmental awareness of the present moment, helping to break the cycle of chronic worry and rumination.

- **Behavioral Activation**: This strategy involves engaging in activities that bring joy and fulfillment, countering the avoidance behaviors and withdrawal that often accompany anxiety.

- **Stress Inoculation Training**: This technique equips individuals with skills to manage stress before it escalates into acute anxiety, incorporating elements of relaxation, cognitive restructuring, and problem-solving.

Incorporating CBT into Daily Routines

For CBT to be truly effective, its principles must be woven into the fabric of daily life:

- **Consistent Practice**: Like any skill, cognitive restructuring and the application of coping strategies require regular practice. This might involve daily journaling, mindfulness practice, or scheduled exposure exercises.

- **Lifestyle Adjustments**: Incorporating regular physical activity, ensuring adequate sleep, and maintaining a balanced diet can enhance the effectiveness of CBT techniques, creating a holistic approach to managing anxiety.

- **Ongoing Learning**: Engaging with CBT-focused resources, such as books, online courses, and workshops, can deepen understanding and commitment to the CBT process.

CBT's comprehensive approach to managing anxiety is both a journey and a commitment. It requires active participation and openness to change, offering a structured path to understanding and reshaping the cognitive and behavioral patterns that underlie anxiety. Through diligent application of CBT techniques and principles, individuals can achieve significant improvements in their anxiety levels, leading to enhanced quality of life and well-being.

Physical Activity: A Natural Anxiety Reducer

The nexus between physical activity and mental health, particularly its efficacy in mitigating symptoms of anxiety, is a domain rich with both scientific inquiry and anecdotal evidence. Exercise, often heralded as a natural antidote to a host of physical ailments, also emerges as a potent, natural anxiety reducer. This dynamic relationship underscores the role of regular physical activity in fostering not only a healthier body but also a more serene mind.

Understanding the Biochemical Impact of Exercise

At the heart of exercise's mood-lifting capabilities is the release of endorphins—neurochemicals produced in the brain that function as natural painkillers and mood elevators. Often referred to as the body's "feel-good" hormones, endorphins are released in response to physical activity, leading to what is commonly known as the "runner's high," a state of euphoria coupled with reduced anxiety and a sense of well-being. This biochemical response not only alleviates immediate symptoms of anxiety but also contributes to long-term improvements in mood and mental health.

In parallel, exercise plays a crucial role in modulating the body's stress hormones, particularly cortisol. While cortisol is an essential element of the body's "fight or flight" response, chronic elevation of cortisol levels can exacerbate anxiety symptoms. Regular exercise helps to regulate cortisol levels, ensuring they rise when needed during stressful situations but don't stay high for too long, which helps prevent the negative effects of long-term stress.

The Psychological Benefits of Exercise

The benefits of exercise transcend biochemical interactions, manifesting profound psychological and emotional enhancements. Physical activity carves out a reprieve from the relentless cycle of anxious thoughts, serving as a constructive diversion that anchors the mind in the here and now. This engenderment of mindfulness during exercise acts as a buffer against anxiety, diluting its intensity and frequency.

Additionally, the role of exercise in fostering self-efficacy and bolstering self-esteem cannot be overstated. The accomplishments felt through meeting or surpassing exercise goals, regardless of their magnitude, ignite a sense of capability and self-assurance. This empowerment is crucial for challenging the sense of helplessness that often shadows anxiety, instilling a mindset equipped to confront and manage anxious thoughts and situations more effectively.

Incorporating Exercise into Daily Life

The incorporation of exercise into daily routines demands a personalized strategy, reflective of one's unique preferences, capacities, and life circumstances. The objective is to identify and embrace forms of physical activity that not only yield the inherent benefits of exercise but also resonate on a personal level, ensuring long-term engagement and adherence.

- **Embracing Incremental Progress**: Initiating an exercise regimen with manageable, modest goals is essential, especially for novices or those reacquainting themselves with physical activity. Simple activities, such as brief walks, can serve as a gateway to experiencing exercise's mood-enhancing benefits.

- **Cultivating Joy in Movement**: The selection of enjoyable activities significantly amplifies the anxiety-mitigating effects of exercise. Whether it's the rhythm of dance, the solitude of hiking, the exhilaration of cycling, or the serenity of yoga, the key lies in pursuing activities that spark intrinsic joy and motivation.

- **Fostering Consistency Through Routine**: The establishment of a consistent exercise schedule is foundational for accruing the long-term benefits of physical activity on anxiety reduction. Identifying specific days, times, and the duration of workouts can facilitate habit formation and adherence.

- **Diversifying Exercise Modalities**: A varied exercise regimen prevents monotony, sustains interest, and addresses different aspects of physical fitness. Alternating between cardiovascular activities, strength training, and flexibility exercises can enrich the exercise experience and optimize health benefits.

- **Setting Attainable Goals**: The articulation of realistic, achievable fitness goals encourages a sense of progression and accomplishment while safeguarding against potential discouragement. Employing the SMART criteria (Specific, Measurable, Attainable, Relevant, Time-bound) can guide goal-setting processes.

- **Leveraging Social Support**: Participating in group exercises or fitness communities can not only enhance motivation through camaraderie and accountability but also reinforce a sense of belonging, further diminishing feelings of isolation often associated with anxiety.

In sum, the synergy between physical activity and anxiety management is both profound and multifaceted, harnessing biochemical, psychological, and social mechanisms to combat anxiety. By embracing physical activity as an integral component of daily life, tailored to one's preferences and lifestyle, individuals can unlock a powerful, natural conduit to improved mental health and overall well-being. This journey towards incorporating exercise into the routine stands as a testament to the enduring power of physical activity in not only sculpting a healthier body but also in cultivating a more peaceful and resilient mind.

Dietary Considerations: Foods That Help and Harm

The relationship between diet and mental health, specifically in the context of anxiety management, is a nuanced field that intersects nutritional science, psychology, and personal health practices. This complex interplay suggests that what we consume can significantly influence our mental state, including the prevalence and intensity of anxiety symptoms. A deeper understanding of how certain foods, nutrients, and dietary patterns affect anxiety can empower individuals to make informed choices that support their mental well-being.

Nutritional Allies in the Battle Against Anxiety

- **Omega-3 Fatty Acids**: The role of omega-3 fatty acids in brain health and anxiety reduction cannot be overstated. These essential fats contribute to the fluidity of cell membranes and are involved in neurotransmitter function, which is crucial for mood regulation. Research indicates that omega-3 supplements can lower anxiety levels, particularly in those with diagnosed disorders. Regular consumption of omega-3-rich foods like fatty fish, walnuts, flaxseeds, and chia seeds is recommended for their mood-stabilizing benefits.

- **Magnesium**: This mineral acts as a cofactor in hundreds of enzymatic processes in the body and is vital for the function of the nervous system. Magnesium deficiency has been linked to heightened anxiety and stress responses. Incorporating magnesium-rich foods such as spinach, almonds, black beans, and whole wheat into daily meals can help mitigate this risk and promote a calmer state of mind.

- **B Vitamins**: The B vitamin complex plays a pivotal role in mental health. Vitamins B6 and B12, in particular, are critical for the synthesis and function of neurotransmitters like serotonin and dopamine, which directly influence mood and anxiety.

Foods such as avocados, poultry, eggs, and leafy greens are excellent sources of B vitamins and can support neurological and psychological health.

- **Antioxidants**: Oxidative stress is a physiological condition that has been implicated in the development and exacerbation of anxiety. Antioxidants neutralize oxidative stress and protect the body and brain from damage. Foods high in antioxidants, such as berries, nuts, dark chocolate, and vegetables, should be integral to an anxiety-reducing diet.

Foods and Substances That May Exacerbate Anxiety

- **Sugar and High-Glycemic Foods**: Eating sugar and high-glycemic carbohydrates can cause quick fluctuations in blood sugar levels, potentially exacerbating or triggering symptoms of anxiety. These fluctuations can cause symptoms such as irritability, fatigue, and jitteriness, mimicking or intensifying feelings of anxiety. Opting for low-glycemic, complex carbohydrates like quinoa, oats, and sweet potatoes can provide more stable energy and mood levels.

- **Caffeine**: As a stimulant, caffeine can exacerbate anxiety symptoms for many individuals by increasing heart rate, blood pressure, and feelings of nervousness. Those prone to anxiety may benefit from reducing caffeine intake or exploring caffeine-free alternatives.

- **Processed and Fried Foods**: Diets high in processed, fried, and fast foods have been associated with an increased risk of depression and anxiety disorders. These foods often contain unhealthy fats, sugars, and additives that can negatively impact brain health and mood. Prioritizing whole, minimally processed foods can enhance overall well-being.

Practical Strategies for Implementing Dietary Changes

- **Holistic Meal Planning**: Integrating anxiety-reducing foods into one's diet requires thoughtful meal planning that encompasses a balance of nutrients. Planning meals and snacks that include omega-3s, magnesium, B vitamins, and antioxidants can ensure a steady intake of these crucial nutrients.

- **Mindful Eating Practices**: Embracing mindful eating can enhance the psychological benefits of meals, encouraging a more present, enjoyable, and stress-free eating experience. This involves paying close attention to the flavors, textures, and sensations of eating, as well as listening to hunger and fullness cues.

- **Staying Hydrated**: Proper hydration is essential for maintaining optimal physiological function and mental clarity. Dehydration can negatively affect mood and cognitive function, potentially increasing feelings of anxiety.

- **Professional Consultation**: For individuals looking to tailor their diet more closely to their mental health needs, consulting with a registered dietitian or nutritionist can provide customized advice and support.

Adopting a diet that supports mental health and reduces anxiety involves more than just individual food choices; it encompasses a holistic approach to eating that prioritizes nutrition, mindfulness, and personal well-being. By making informed, conscious decisions about dietary habits, individuals can leverage the power of nutrition to combat anxiety, promoting a healthier, more balanced state of mind.

CHAPTER 3

BUILDING RESILIENCE AGAINST ANXIETY

This chapter delves into focusing on cultivating inner strength to confront life's challenges head-on. It underscores the importance of establishing a supportive network, setting and respecting personal boundaries, and the role of consistent routines in fostering stability. Additionally, it introduces effective stress management strategies and highlights the value of embracing change. These components work synergistically to bolster resilience, equipping you to navigate through anxiety with confidence and grace.

Establishing a Support System

Establishing a robust support system is pivotal in navigating the complexities of anxiety, offering a lifeline through emotional, practical, and professional support. This intricate process involves a detailed exploration of current relationships, communication strategies, and the pursuit of new connections that resonate with one's needs for understanding and empathy. A well-rounded support network not only provides a safety net during challenging times but also enhances overall resilience and mental well-being.

Evaluating and Strengthening Existing Relationships

The foundation of building a support system begins with an introspective look at one's current relationships. This evaluation requires considering which individuals consistently provide a sense of safety, understanding, and positive reinforcement. It's essential to identify those who are empathetic listeners, offer constructive feedback, and respect your boundaries.

- **Initiating Conversations**: Opening up about anxiety is a significant step that demands vulnerability and trust. Approach these conversations with honesty and clarity, expressing your feelings, experiences, and what form of support you're seeking. It's also crucial to communicate your boundaries regarding the discussion of your anxiety, ensuring these conversations remain helpful and not overwhelming.

- **Reciprocity in Relationships**: True support systems are built on mutual respect and aid. Show willingness to support others, recognizing that shared experiences can deepen bonds and foster a sense of belonging. This reciprocity ensures that the support system is sustainable and rooted in genuine care and understanding.

Expanding Your Support Network

For many, existing relationships may not fully address the spectrum of support needed to manage anxiety. Expanding one's network to include new connections or professionals can fill these gaps.

- **Community Engagement**: Local community groups, clubs, or organizations related to personal interests or mental health can offer new opportunities for connection. Participation in such groups provides a platform for sharing experiences and receiving support from individuals who understand the journey through anxiety.

- **Online Support Networks**: The digital age offers unprecedented access to global communities where individuals can find others with similar experiences. Online forums, social media groups, and mental health platforms can provide valuable resources, advice, and a sense of community. Engaging in these spaces requires discernment to ensure that interactions are positive and constructive.

- **Seeking Professional Help**: Mental health professionals, including psychologists, psychiatrists, and counselors, are invaluable members of a support system. They offer not only therapeutic support but also guidance on building coping strategies and managing anxiety. Initiating contact with such professionals may involve referrals, researching local mental health services, or exploring teletherapy options.

Nurturing Supportive Connections

Building a support system is an ongoing process that involves more than just establishing connections; it requires nurturing and maintaining these relationships.

- **Frequent Communication**: Regular check-ins with members of your support network help keep the lines of communication open. These interactions can range from sharing daily experiences to discussing deeper feelings related to anxiety.

- **Group Activities**: Organizing or participating in group activities can strengthen relationships within your support network. Whether it's a casual meetup, a shared hobby, or a group therapy session, these activities foster a sense of community and shared experience.

- **Education and Awareness**: Educating those within your support system about anxiety can enhance their ability to provide meaningful support. Sharing articles, books, or resources about anxiety can help friends and family understand your experiences and how best to support you.

Embracing Vulnerability and Mutual Understanding

At the heart of expanding and maintaining a support system is the willingness to be vulnerable. This openness fosters deeper connections, built on trust and mutual understanding. It's through vulnerability that relationships grow stronger, providing a foundation of support that can weather the challenges of anxiety.

In crafting a support system, individuals empower themselves with a network of allies dedicated to their well-being. Through careful evaluation of existing relationships, open communication, seeking new connections, and ongoing engagement, a support system becomes a cornerstone of resilience against anxiety. This comprehensive approach not only aids in managing anxiety but also enriches one's life with meaningful, supportive relationships.

Creating and Maintaining Healthy Boundaries

In the realm of personal well-being and mental health, the establishment and maintenance of healthy boundaries stand as crucial practices for managing stress and anxiety. These boundaries, both tangible and intangible, serve as vital parameters within which individuals navigate their interactions, safeguarding their emotional health and ensuring their relationships are mutually respectful and enriching.

Foundations of Healthy Boundaries

At their core, healthy boundaries are the expression of one's values, limits, and needs, articulated clearly to others. They are essential for emotional well-being, serving to delineate the space between personal autonomy and communal or relational engagement. Boundaries can encompass a wide range of interactions and aspects of life, including physical space, emotional intimacy, intellectual boundaries, and time management.

Identifying Personal and Emotional Limits

The journey to establishing boundaries begins with a thorough self-assessment to discern one's comfort levels, triggers, and non-negotiables in various contexts.

- **Self-reflection**: Engage in regular self-reflection to understand your emotional responses, triggers, and sources of discomfort. Journals, mindfulness practices, and therapy can facilitate this introspective process.

- **Define Your Values**: Clarify your core values and principles. Understanding what matters most to you can guide the setting of boundaries that reflect and protect these values.

- **Recognize Physical and Emotional Needs**: Acknowledge and prioritize your physical and emotional needs, such as the need for solitude, social interaction, physical affection, or intellectual stimulation.

Communicating Boundaries Effectively

The articulation of boundaries to others is a delicate process that requires clarity, assertiveness, and respect for the relationship dynamic.

- **Choose the Appropriate Setting**: Initiate conversations about boundaries in a neutral, private setting where both parties are calm and open to dialogue.

- **Be Clear and Specific**: Avoid vagueness. Clearly describe the boundary, why it's important to you, and how its respect or violation impacts you emotionally.

- **Practice Assertive Communication**: Assertiveness involves expressing your thoughts and feelings confidently and respectfully, without aggression or passivity. It's about respecting both your needs and those of others.

Upholding Boundaries Amid Challenges

Maintaining established boundaries often involves navigating feelings of guilt, fear of rejection, or pressure from others to conform to their expectations.

- **Self-affirmation**: Reinforce your right to set boundaries through positive self-affirmation. Remind yourself that prioritizing your well-being is not only necessary but a sign of self-respect.

- **Prepare for Resistance**: Anticipate and plan for potential pushback. Having a response strategy can help you remain firm and composed when your boundaries are challenged.

- **Seek Support**: Lean on your support system for encouragement and advice when facing difficulties in maintaining your boundaries.

Navigating Common Boundary Challenges

Maintaining healthy boundaries can evoke complex emotions and reactions, both internally and from others.

- **Managing Guilt**: Guilt can arise from asserting one's needs, especially if accustomed to prioritizing others' needs. Recognizing this guilt as a natural but surmountable reaction is key to reinforcing your boundaries.

- **Addressing Pushback**: Resistance from others, particularly those unaccustomed to your boundaries, can be distressing. Consistent reinforcement, coupled with open communication about the importance of these boundaries, is critical.

The Transformative Impact of Healthy Boundaries

Well-defined and respected boundaries have profound implications for personal well-being and the quality of one's relationships.

- **Enhanced Mental Health**: Boundaries reduce stress and anxiety by preventing emotional overextension and respecting personal limits, leading to improved mental health and resilience.

- **Improved Relationships**: By clearly articulating needs and expectations, boundaries foster healthier, more transparent relationships built on mutual respect and understanding.

- **Increased Self-Esteem and Agency**: Successfully establishing and maintaining boundaries bolsters self-esteem and a sense of personal agency, affirming one's ability to protect and prioritize personal well-being.

The path to creating and maintaining healthy boundaries is a dynamic and ongoing process, marked by self-discovery, assertive communication, and continuous adjustment to changing needs and circumstances. While challenges are inevitable, the pursuit of healthy boundaries is a testament to one's commitment to personal well-being and the cultivation of meaningful, respectful relationships. Through this dedicated practice, individuals empower themselves to navigate life with confidence, knowing they possess the tools to protect their emotional health and foster positive interactions.

The Power of Routine in Building Resilience

The stabilizing power of a well-structured daily routine in fostering resilience, especially under the duress of stress or uncertainty, is a principle deeply rooted in both psychological research and practical wisdom. Routines establish a rhythm to our days, imparting a predictable structure that can significantly alleviate the cognitive load of decision-making and adaptively channel our mental resources. This strategic organization of daily activities not only optimizes productivity and well-being but also serves as a bulwark against the destabilizing forces of anxiety and stress, thereby bolstering our mental resilience.

Underpinning the Stabilizing Effect of Routine

At its essence, a routine is a sequence of habits that provides a framework for daily life. This framework reduces the mental strain associated with planning and decision-making by creating a predictable flow of activities. In doing so, it diminishes the ambient levels of stress and frees up cognitive resources for coping with unforeseen challenges or for engaging in more complex problem-solving tasks.

Constructing a Balanced Routine

The architecture of a resilient-enhancing routine requires a holistic consideration of one's physical, emotional, and social needs. Here's a deeper exploration into achieving this equilibrium:

- **Holistic Activity Integration**: A resilient routine harmonizes time allocated for work and productivity with moments dedicated to relaxation and pursuits that evoke joy. This equilibrium fosters a sense of fulfillment and prevents the erosion of well-being through overwork or monotony.

- **Strategic Socialization**: Human beings are inherently social creatures. Incorporating regular, meaningful interactions within one's routine combats loneliness and nurtures a supportive community, crucial for mental health.

- **Physical Activity as a Pillar**: The inclusion of exercise not only supports physical health but also acts as a powerful antidote to stress, thanks to the release of endorphins. Embedding physical activity within one's daily routine can range from dedicated workout sessions to integrating more movement into daily tasks.

- **Prioritizing Restorative Rest**: Ensuring adequate rest is foundational to resilience. Quality sleep and planned breaks rejuvenate the mind and body, enabling better stress management and cognitive function.

Adapting Routines Amidst Flux

Life's dynamic nature necessitates that our routines possess an inherent flexibility, allowing them to evolve in response to changing circumstances while still providing a scaffold of stability.

- **Embracing Flexibility with Intent**: View changes as opportunities to reassess and refine your routine rather than as disruptions. Maintaining core elements that anchor your routine can help preserve its benefits even as adjustments are made.

- **Developing Contingency Plans**: Anticipate potential disruptions and devise alternative plans. This proactive approach ensures continuity in your routine's protective and stabilizing effects.

Navigating Routine Maintenance Challenges

Despite their benefits, establishing and adhering to routines can sometimes be daunting due to various barriers such as procrastination, external disruptions, or the inertia of old habits.

- **Incremental Implementation**: Tackling too many changes at once can be overwhelming. Introduce new elements gradually, building on each success to foster sustainable habits.

- **Leveraging Environmental Cues**: Anchor new habits to specific cues in your environment or schedule to enhance their stickiness. Consistency in context can significantly bolster habit formation.

- **Fostering Accountability**: Sharing your goals and progress with someone supportive can increase your motivation and commitment, providing an external source of encouragement and accountability.

The Transformative Impact of Routine on Resilience

A thoughtfully curated routine transcends mere time management—it's a lifestyle strategy that enhances personal agency and equips individuals to face adversities with grace. By meticulously organizing our days, we not only optimize our individual capacities for productivity and joy but also fortify our psychological resilience. The sense of control and competence fostered by a reliable routine mitigates the impact of stress and cultivates a proactive, rather than reactive, approach to life's challenges.

Moreover, the social and emotional connections strengthened through routine activities contribute to a support network that is invaluable in times of need. As we navigate the complexities of modern life, the intentional creation, and maintenance of a balanced routine stand as a testament to our commitment to holistic well-being and resilience.

In conclusion, the deliberate crafting and diligent upholding of a balanced daily routine is a profound exercise in resilience building. Through the strategic allocation of time for work, relaxation, social connections, physical activity, and rest, individuals can create a life framework that not only supports optimal functioning but also provides a bulwark against the vicissitudes of life. As we refine our routines in response to life's inevitable changes, we learn the art of adaptability, ensuring that our routines remain a source of strength and stability, irrespective of external pressures. This journey toward an optimized and adaptable routine underscores the indelible link between structured daily habits and our capacity to thrive in an ever-changing environment.

Stress Management Strategies

Effective stress management is a multi-faceted endeavor, crucial for safeguarding mental well-being and enhancing life quality. This comprehensive exploration delves into a variety of stress management techniques, spanning from immediate interventions for acute stress episodes to sustained strategies aimed at reducing chronic stress. Understanding the mechanisms, benefits, and practical applications of each technique is essential for anyone seeking to navigate stress with agility and resilience. Additionally, this guide offers insights into crafting a personalized stress management plan that aligns with individual lifestyle preferences and stressors, encouraging a holistic and adaptive approach to stress mitigation.

Decoding Stress: Its Dynamics and Impacts

Stress, characterized by the body's response to perceived threats or demands, manifests in both positive and negative forms. While acute stress can catalyze motivation and focus, chronic stress, left unchecked, precipitates a host of adverse physical and psychological outcomes, underscoring the imperative for effective management strategies.

Acute Stress Relief Techniques

- **Focused Breathing Techniques**: Techniques such as the 4-7-8 method, diaphragmatic breathing, and box breathing offer quick, accessible means to invoke the body's relaxation response, mitigating the immediate sensations of stress.

- **Progressive Muscle Relaxation (PMR)**: By systematically tensing and relaxing different muscle groups, PMR helps identify and release the physical manifestations of stress, offering a path to bodily and mental relaxation.

- **Brief Mindfulness Practices**: Engaging in short-term mindfulness exercises or guided meditations can anchor the mind in the present moment, curtailing the cycle of stress-inducing thoughts and rumination.

Long-term Stress Reduction Strategies

- **Consistent Physical Activity**: Incorporating regular exercise into one's routine not only expends the excess energy triggered by the stress response but also fosters endorphin release, enhancing mood and stress resilience over time. A varied exercise regimen, from aerobic activities to strength training and yoga, ensures comprehensive benefits.

- **Creative Expression**: Creative pursuits offer a therapeutic outlet for processing and expressing emotions, mitigating stress through distraction and engagement. Whether through art, music, writing, or dance, these activities foster emotional release and joy.

- **Effective Time Management** : Using effective time management techniques can greatly alleviate the stress related to deadlines and having too much to do in a schedule. Prioritizing tasks, setting achievable goals, and employing organizational tools can streamline workload management and alleviate stress.

Crafting a Tailored Stress Management Plan

Personalization is key to an effective stress management plan. Consideration of personal preferences, daily routines, and specific stress triggers is essential in developing a strategy that is both practical and impactful.

- **Comprehensive Stressor Analysis**: Maintaining a stress journal can illuminate patterns and triggers, facilitating targeted interventions and proactive stress management.

- **Diverse Technique Integration**: A balanced approach, combining immediate stress relief methods with long-term lifestyle adjustments, ensures a robust defense against stress. This might include daily mindfulness practice alongside weekly physical activities and creative hobbies.

- **Incremental Goal Setting**: Establishing small, manageable objectives encourages the gradual integration of stress management practices into daily life, enhancing the likelihood of adherence and long-term success.

- **Community and Support Engagement**: Building a support network of individuals who share or support your stress management goals can provide encouragement, accountability, and shared experiences, enriching the journey towards stress resilience.

Navigating Challenges in Stress Management

The path to effective stress management is often fraught with obstacles, from maintaining motivation to adapting strategies in the face of life changes.

- **Ensuring Routine Adherence**: Integrating stress management practices into daily life demands discipline and motivation. Establishing routines, setting reminders, and creating accountability mechanisms can bolster consistency and engagement.

- **Adaptive Flexibility**: Life's unpredictability necessitates a flexible approach to stress management. Being open to modifying one's routine in response to new stressors or changing circumstances ensures sustained effectiveness and relevance of stress management strategies.

- **Exploratory Persistence**: Discovering the most effective stress management techniques is a personal and evolving process.

Experimentation, patience, and openness to trying new approaches are crucial for identifying the best fit for individual needs and preferences.

In crafting a detailed and adaptive approach to stress management, individuals empower themselves with the tools necessary to navigate the complexities of stress with resilience and grace. Through the strategic application of both short-term and long-term techniques, coupled with a commitment to personalization and consistency, it's possible to not only mitigate the impacts of stress but also to thrive amidst life's challenges, enhancing overall well-being and quality of life.

Embracing Change: Adapting to New Challenges

Embracing change and navigating new challenges are undeniably central to personal growth and resilience. The dynamism of life ensures that change is a constant, yet it frequently stirs deep-seated anxieties and fears within us. This is largely due to the human psyche's preference for stability and predictability, elements that are often disrupted during periods of transition. However, adopting a perspective that views change not as an insurmountable threat but as a fertile ground for development and renewal can significantly alter one's experience of these transitions.

Understanding Change and Its Complex Dynamics

Change, whether it's expected or comes out of the blue, challenges our sense of security and control over our environment. It forces us out of our comfort zones, demanding adaptations that can seem daunting at first glance. The anxiety that accompanies change is rooted in the fear of the unknown and the potential loss of what is familiar and comfortable. Yet, it's important to recognize that change also catalyzes personal evolution, pushing individuals to develop new skills, reassess their values, and deepen their understanding of themselves and the world around them.

The Essence of Psychological Flexibility

Psychological flexibility is the cornerstone of successfully adapting to change. It embodies the capacity to remain fluid in one's thoughts and actions, responding to life's shifts with grace rather than rigidity. This skill encompasses several key components:

- **Embracing Openness and Curiosity**: Cultivating a mindset of openness involves welcoming new experiences without preconceived judgments or expectations. It encourages an attitude of curiosity, where change is approached as a series of questions to be explored rather than problems to be solved.

- **Mindfulness and Presence**: The practice of mindfulness enhances one's ability to stay grounded in the present moment, despite the uncertainties that change might bring. This presence of mind allows individuals to observe their thoughts and feelings about change without becoming overwhelmed by them.

- **Aligned Action with Core Values**: Understanding and acting in accordance with one's core values provides a compass during times of change, guiding decisions and actions that resonate with deeper personal principles.

Developing Skills for Psychological Flexibility

To cultivate psychological flexibility, individuals can engage in several practical exercises:

- **Mindfulness Meditation**: Regular meditation practices encourage a state of awareness and acceptance of the present moment, fostering a non-judgmental relationship with one's thoughts and feelings.

- **Cognitive Defusion Techniques**: These strategies involve distancing oneself from the content of one's thoughts, recognizing them as mere mental events rather than objective truths about oneself or reality.

- **Exploring Personal Values**: Through reflective exercises, individuals can clarify their core values, which serve as anchors and guides in navigating the seas of change.

Inspirational Examples of Adaptation

The stories of those who have successfully navigated significant life changes offer valuable lessons and inspiration:

- **Entrepreneurial Shifts**: Consider the entrepreneur who pivots their business model in response to market changes. This adaptation, though fraught with uncertainty, opens up new avenues for innovation and success, demonstrating the power of strategic flexibility.

- **Personal Transformations**: The journey of an individual who embarks on a path of self-discovery after a major life event, such as a career change or the end of a relationship, illustrates the transformative potential of embracing change. By remaining open to new experiences and self-reflection, they uncover new passions and a deeper sense of purpose.

Strategies for Proactively Embracing Change

- **Foster a Growth Mindset**: View change as an opportunity for learning and growth. Adopt the belief that abilities and understanding can be developed through dedication and hard work.

- **Build a Resilient Support System**:
- Nurture connections with individuals who encourage your personal development and flexibility. A strong network can provide encouragement, advice, and different perspectives.

- **Reflect on Past Adaptations**: Reminisce about previous instances where you successfully navigated change. This reflection can boost confidence in your ability to handle future transitions.

- **Practice Gratitude**: Focus on the positive aspects and opportunities that change can bring. Gratitude can shift your perspective, making the challenges of change seem more manageable.

In sum, the journey toward embracing change and adapting to new challenges is enriched by developing psychological flexibility, seeking inspiration from successful adaptations, and employing targeted strategies to approach change with a sense of curiosity and openness. This comprehensive approach not only facilitates a smoother transition through the uncertainties of change but also catalyzes personal growth, leading to a more adaptable, resilient, and fulfilling life.

CHAPTER 4

ADVANCED STRATEGIES FOR LONG-TERM WELLNESS

This chapter unfolds a comprehensive guide to maintaining and enhancing mental well-being through a deeper exploration of nuanced wellness strategies. It covers advanced meditation techniques that foster profound relaxation, examines the benefits and considerations of diverse professional therapy options, and demystifies the role and effects of medication in the treatment of mental health conditions. Additionally, it provides invaluable insights into preventing relapse and keeping anxiety at bay, alongside practical advice for integrating effective wellness practices into everyday life, aiming for a balanced and holistic approach to enduring health and happiness.

Advanced Meditation Techniques for Deep Relaxation

Diving into the depths of advanced meditation techniques reveals a world where profound relaxation and mental clarity are not just aspirations but attainable states of being. Among the myriad of practices, Zazen and Transcendental Meditation (TM) stand out as beacons for those seeking to transcend the turbulence of anxiety and the incessant chatter of the mind. These methodologies, supported by a rich tapestry of scientific research and personal testimonies, offer not just a temporary respite but a transformative journey toward sustained well-being.

Zazen: The Zen of Seated Meditation

Zazen, a cornerstone of Zen Buddhism, emphasizes seated meditation as a means to achieve deep mental stillness and insight. Unlike meditation practices that focus on a specific object or thought, Zazen encourages practitioners to sit in quiet observation, letting thoughts and sensations arise and pass without attachment or judgment.

Technique and Practice

- **Finding the Seat**: The physical posture in Zazen is paramount. Traditionally, practitioners sit on a zafu (cushion) in the full or half-lotus position, though a chair can be used for those for whom this is uncomfortable. The key is an upright, stable posture that allows for deep breathing and alertness.

- **The Position of Hands and Eyes**: The hands form the cosmic mudra, resting on the lap with palms upward and thumbs lightly touching, symbolizing the interconnectedness of all things. The eyes remain slightly open, gazing softly downward, to maintain the connection with the external world without getting drawn into distractions.

- **Breath and Mind**: Breath in Zazen is natural and unforced, with attention placed on the gentle rise and fall of the abdomen. Practitioners observe thoughts and sensations as they arise and pass, without engagement or attachment, embodying the fluidity and impermanence of experience.

Scientific Support and Benefits

Research underscores Zazen's efficacy in reducing stress and anxiety, highlighting its impact on lowering blood pressure, enhancing concentration, and fostering a state of equanimity. By cultivating a non-judgmental awareness, practitioners learn to detach from habitual patterns of anxiety and stress, opening pathways to deeper insight and inner peace.

Transcendental Meditation: The Journey Beyond Thought

Transcendental Meditation is a technique that utilizes a personal mantra as a focal point to transcend the surface level of the mind, reaching a state of pure consciousness. This practice, typically taught by certified instructors, involves silently repeating a mantra, allowing the practitioner to experience deeper levels of awareness beyond ordinary thinking.

Technique and Implementation

- **Personalized Instruction**: The initiation into TM is through one-on-one instruction with a certified teacher, ensuring a mantra tailored to the individual's essence and life path.

- **Regular Practice**: The cornerstone of TM is its twice-daily practice, each session lasting 20 minutes. This regularity is crucial for delving deeper into transcendental states and reaping the cumulative benefits over time.

- **Mantra Repetition**: The gentle, silent repetition of the mantra serves as a focal point, effortlessly drawing the mind away from surface-level distractions and into a state of profound relaxation and alertness.

Research Findings

Studies on TM have documented its positive effects on mental health, including significant reductions in anxiety, depression, and PTSD symptoms. Furthermore, TM has been shown to improve cognitive functions, creativity, and problem-solving abilities, making it a powerful tool for personal and professional growth.

Incorporating Advanced Practices into Daily Life

Adopting Zazen or TM into one's lifestyle requires intention and adaptability. Gradually increasing practice duration and maintaining consistency are vital. Equally important is the integration of the meditative mindset into daily activities, fostering mindfulness and presence throughout the day.

Personal Accounts and Transformative Effects

Real-world accounts of individuals who have embraced these meditation practices illuminate their transformative potential. From executives finding solace and clarity amidst corporate chaos to artists tapping into new wellsprings of creativity, the stories are as diverse as they are inspiring. These narratives underscore the universality of meditation's benefits, transcending cultural, professional, and personal boundaries.

In conclusion, advanced meditation techniques like Zazen and Transcendental Meditation offer profound avenues for achieving deep relaxation, enhancing mental health, and fostering a resilient, adaptable approach to life's inevitable changes. By understanding the nuances of these practices, supported by scientific evidence and enriched by personal experiences, individuals are empowered to embark on a journey of self-discovery and transformation. The path of meditation is one of continual learning and exploration, where each step forward reveals new horizons of well-being and insight.

Exploring Professional Therapy Options

Navigating the landscape of professional therapy for anxiety management can be both a journey of discovery and a pathway to profound personal growth. Modern psychology offers a variety of therapeutic approaches, each with its unique framework for understanding and treating anxiety. Among these, Cognitive-

Behavioral Therapy (CBT) and Acceptance and Commitment Therapy (ACT) stand out for their effectiveness and widespread adoption. This detailed exploration aims to unpack the methodologies, processes, and real-life impacts of these therapies, providing insights into their practice and offering practical advice for those considering therapy as a step toward wellness.

Cognitive-Behavioral Therapy (CBT)

Cognitive Behavioral Therapy (CBT) is a proven and highly successful method for addressing anxiety disorders, backed by substantial evidence. It operates on the principle that negative thought patterns and behaviors are not just symptoms of anxiety but also contributors to its maintenance.

Methodology and Process

- **Identifying Negative Thought Patterns**: CBT begins with the identification of negative thought patterns (cognitive distortions) that contribute to anxiety. Therapists work with clients to recognize thoughts that are irrational, overly critical, or doom-focused.

- **Challenging and Changing Thoughts**: Through techniques like cognitive restructuring, clients learn to challenge these thoughts and replace them with more balanced and realistic ones. This process requires active participation and practice.

- **Behavioral Experiments**: CBT also involves changing behaviors that reinforce anxiety, through exposure therapy or gradual engagement with feared situations, helping to reduce avoidance behaviors.

Duration and Success Stories

Typically, CBT is conducted over a series of sessions, often ranging from 5 to 20, depending on the individual's needs and progress. Success stories abound, with many individuals experiencing significant reductions in anxiety symptoms, improved coping skills, and enhanced quality of life. For instance, a person with social anxiety might learn to identify and change their belief that "everyone is judging me" to a more realistic understanding of social interactions, reducing anxiety over time.

Acceptance and Commitment Therapy (ACT)

ACT offers a unique perspective on managing anxiety, emphasizing acceptance of negative thoughts and feelings as an alternative to struggling against them, coupled with a commitment to actions aligned with personal values.

Framework and Implementation

- **Acceptance**: ACT teaches clients to observe their thoughts without judgment, recognizing them as transient mental events rather than facts. This mindful acceptance helps to decrease the struggle with unwanted thoughts and feelings.

- **Commitment to Action**: Concurrently, ACT focuses on identifying personal values and committing to behavior changes that promote these values, even in the presence of anxiety. This might involve setting goals that are meaningful to the individual and taking steps towards these goals, despite feelings of anxiety.

Duration and Real-life Impact

ACT therapy can vary in length, often tailored to the individual's needs and progress, with some experiencing significant benefits within a relatively short timeframe. Stories from individuals who have undergone ACT highlight its transformative impact, such as a person finding the courage to pursue a long-desired career path by accepting their fear of failure while committing to actions that reflect their core values of growth and learning.

Navigating the Therapist Selection Process

The therapeutic alliance, or the relationship between therapist and client, is a critical determinant of therapy's success. Selecting the right therapist, therefore, is a vital step.

Considerations for Choosing a Therapist

- **Specialization and Experience**: Seek therapists with specialized training in CBT or ACT and experience in treating anxiety disorders. Many therapists provide detailed profiles of their expertise online or during initial consultations.

- **Therapeutic Approach and Style**: Understand the therapist's approach to treatment and ensure it aligns with your preferences for structure, collaboration, and the types of techniques used.

- **Cultural and Personal Compatibility**: Consider factors like cultural background, language, and personal compatibility. A therapist who understands and respects your unique context can significantly enhance the therapeutic experience.

- **Logistics and Practicalities**: Evaluate logistical aspects such as location, session availability, and insurance coverage. Many therapists now offer teletherapy options, broadening access to care.

Embarking on the Therapeutic Journey

Embarking on therapy is a commitment to oneself—a step towards understanding and managing anxiety through proven strategies and the guidance of a skilled therapist. Whether through the structured path of CBT or the value-oriented approach of ACT, therapy offers a transformative potential for individuals ready to engage deeply with their mental health. Armed with comprehensive knowledge about these therapeutic modalities and guided by thoughtful consideration in selecting a therapist, individuals are well-equipped to navigate the complexities of anxiety and move towards a future defined by resilience, clarity, and personal growth.

Medication: Understanding Its Role and Effects

In the multifaceted journey of anxiety management, medication stands as a critical pillar alongside psychotherapy and lifestyle modifications. Its role is not just to alleviate symptoms but to restore a sense of normalcy and well-being, enabling individuals to fully engage in life and therapeutic practices.

Understanding Medication's Role in Comprehensive Anxiety Management

Medications for anxiety are designed to address various biochemical imbalances that contribute to anxiety disorders. Their use is often recommended for individuals experiencing significant distress or functional impairment due to anxiety. Medications can provide a stabilizing effect, reducing symptoms to a manageable level and allowing individuals to participate more effectively in therapy and daily activities.

Navigating the Decision-Making Process

The decision to incorporate medication into anxiety management is multifaceted, requiring a careful evaluation of the individual's unique circumstances, including the severity of symptoms, personal health history, and specific diagnosis.

- **Diagnosis and Evaluation**: Accurate diagnosis is paramount, as different anxiety disorders may respond better to different medications. A comprehensive assessment by a psychiatrist or primary care provider familiar with mental health conditions can identify the most appropriate treatment plan.

- **Personal Health History and Preferences**: A detailed discussion of the individual's health history, including any pre-existing conditions, allergies, and past experiences with medications, guides the selection process. Personal preferences and concerns should also be considered, ensuring that the chosen medication aligns with the individual's values and treatment goals.

- **Educating on Side Effects and Expectations**: Understanding the potential side effects and how they might impact daily life is crucial. Healthcare providers should offer clear, accessible information, allowing for informed consent and active participation in the treatment decision.

Common Medications for Anxiety and Their Mechanisms

Several classes of medications are used in treating anxiety, each working through different mechanisms:

- **Selective Serotonin Reuptake Inhibitors (SSRIs)** and **Serotonin-Norepinephrine Reuptake Inhibitors (SNRIs)** increase levels of neurotransmitters in the brain, contributing to mood regulation and have been found effective across various anxiety disorders.

- **Benzodiazepines** offer immediate relief from acute anxiety symptoms by enhancing the effect of the neurotransmitter GABA, promoting relaxation. Due to dependency risks, their use is typically limited to short-term or as-needed bases.

- **Buspirone** and **Beta-Blockers** are used in specific cases, such as persistent generalized anxiety or performance anxiety, respectively. Buspirone acts on serotonin receptors, while beta-blockers block the effects of adrenaline, reducing physical symptoms of anxiety.

The Collaborative Approach to Medication Management

Successful medication management relies on ongoing collaboration between the individual and their healthcare team. This includes regular monitoring of symptoms, side effects, and overall well-being, allowing for timely adjustments to the treatment plan.

- **Monitoring and Adjustments**: Regular follow-ups to assess the medication's effectiveness and adjust dosages or switch medications as necessary are key to finding the optimal therapeutic regimen.

- **Addressing Side Effects**: Open discussions about side effects ensure that any adverse reactions are promptly managed, maintaining the individual's quality of life.

- **Holistic Care Considerations**: Medication is often one component of a broader treatment plan. Integrating medication with psychotherapy, lifestyle changes, and other interventions provides a holistic approach to anxiety management.

Real-Life Success Stories: The Impact of Appropriate Medication

Maria, a 34-year-old graphic designer, faced debilitating social anxiety that hindered her career progression and personal relationships. Her fear of judgment in social settings led her to decline job opportunities and avoid gatherings, leaving her feeling isolated and stagnant. After years of struggling, Maria sought help from a psychiatrist who diagnosed her with social anxiety disorder and recommended a combination of Cognitive-Behavioral Therapy (CBT) and an SSRI (Selective Serotonin Reuptake Inhibitor).

Initially hesitant about medication, Maria decided to give it a try, motivated by her desire for change. Within a few weeks of starting the SSRI, she noticed a significant reduction in her anxiety levels. Social situations became less daunting, allowing her to engage more freely and confidently with colleagues and friends. The medication, in conjunction with ongoing CBT, provided Maria with the tools to challenge and change her negative thought patterns related to social interactions.

Encouraged by her progress, Maria accepted a leadership position at her firm, a role she would have declined in the past due to her anxiety. Her story illustrates the transformative impact of appropriate medication when combined with therapy, empowering her to overcome barriers imposed by social anxiety and pursue a fulfilling career and richer personal life.

Choosing the Right Therapist and Medication: Tips and Considerations

- **Research and Referrals**: Seeking referrals from trusted healthcare providers or recommendations from trusted sources can help in finding a psychiatrist or therapist experienced in treating anxiety disorders.
- **Questions to Ask**: Inquiring about the provider's experience with specific medications, their approach to managing side effects, and their philosophy regarding medication and therapy can offer insights into their suitability.

- **Assessing Compatibility**: Feeling comfortable and understood by the healthcare provider is crucial for a successful therapeutic relationship. Initial consultations can help gauge this compatibility.

In embracing medication as part of anxiety management, individuals embark on a journey toward reclaiming their lives from the grip of anxiety. Through informed decision-making, collaborative care, and personalized treatment plans, medication can significantly contribute to the comprehensive management of anxiety, facilitating both immediate relief and long-term wellness.

Preventing Relapse: Keeping Anxiety at Bay

Preventing relapse in the journey of managing anxiety is akin to navigating through uncharted waters with a compass—the compass being the strategies and skills acquired during treatment. Maintaining the gains made through therapy and medication requires vigilance, self-awareness, and a commitment to continuous self-care. This detailed exploration delves into the critical aspects of relapse prevention, offering practical guidance for sustaining long-term wellness and resilience against anxiety.

Recognizing Early Warning Signs

Effectively preventing relapse begins with the nuanced understanding and recognition of early warning signs. These signs are the body and mind's preliminary alerts that anxiety levels may be escalating beyond one's typical baseline. They can manifest as psychological cues, such as excessive worrying about future events, feeling on edge or irritable without a clear cause, and experiencing intrusive thoughts or panic attacks. Physically, signs may include increased heart rate, sweating, trembling, or insomnia.

Regular Self-Monitoring: The Foundation of Awareness

The practice of regularly tracking your mood, anxiety levels, and potential stressors is invaluable for early detection of relapse signs.

- **Journaling**: Start with a daily journal to document your emotional and mental state. Use it to note changes in your mood, specific anxiety levels, and circumstances or thoughts that might have triggered these changes. This practice can help you identify patterns over time, offering insights into your anxiety triggers and the effectiveness of your coping strategies.

- **Digital Tools**: Consider utilizing digital apps designed for mood tracking. Many offer features like trend analysis, reminders, and personalized insights, which can augment your self-monitoring efforts.

Mindfulness Practices: Enhancing Early Warning Detection

Incorporating mindfulness into your daily routine can significantly improve your awareness of your mental state, helping you recognize early signs of anxiety.

- **Daily Mindfulness Meditation**: Dedicate time each day to mindfulness meditation. Begin with a brief period and progressively extend the length over time. Focus on your breath or perform body scans to cultivate presence and awareness.

- **Mindfulness in Daily Activities**: Practice mindfulness during routine activities. Whether eating, walking, or working, fully immerse yourself in the experience, paying close attention to your senses and any arising thoughts or feelings.

Developing a Personalized Relapse Prevention Plan

A robust relapse prevention plan is personalized, comprehensive, and flexible. It encompasses understanding triggers, having a list of coping strategies at the ready, and knowing when and how to seek help.

Components of an Effective Plan

- **Trigger Identification**: Understanding what situations, thoughts, or feelings trigger anxiety is crucial. This awareness enables individuals to prepare or avoid certain triggers when possible.

- **Coping Strategies**: List effective coping strategies learned in therapy, such as deep breathing, cognitive restructuring, or engaging in physical activity. This list serves as a quick reference during times of heightened anxiety.

- **Wellness Activities**: Incorporate regular wellness activities that promote overall mental health, such as exercise, healthy eating, adequate sleep, and hobbies that bring joy.

- **Emergency Contacts**: Have a list of contacts, including therapists, supportive family members, or friends, and crisis hotlines, to reach out to when feeling overwhelmed.

- **Regular Reviews**: Periodically review and adjust the plan as needed. Recovery and relapse prevention are dynamic processes that evolve with time.

Staying Connected with Support Systems

The role of a supportive network, whether it consists of healthcare professionals, family, friends, or support groups, cannot be overstated. Regular check-ins with these supports can provide encouragement, perspective, and accountability.

Revisiting Therapy

- In some cases, revisiting therapy sessions can reinforce coping mechanisms or address new challenges. Whether it's a "booster" session with a cognitive-behavioral therapist or joining a support group, staying engaged with therapeutic resources is vital.

Inspiring Stories of Navigating Potential Relapses

Personal anecdotes serve as beacons of hope and resilience, demonstrating that navigating through potential relapses is not only possible but also an opportunity for further growth.

Emma's Journey Through Anxiety Management

Emma's journey through the intricacies of managing generalized anxiety disorder encapsulates the resilience and determination intrinsic to the human spirit. At 28, having carved a successful career in software development, Emma found solace and stability in the routines and coping strategies she had developed through dedicated therapy sessions and medication management. Her progress was tangible, marked by fewer panic attacks, a newfound ability to engage in social settings without the overwhelming cloud of anxiety, and an overall sense of control over her mental health. Yet, life, with its inherent unpredictability, presented Emma with a formidable challenge that threatened to disrupt the equilibrium she had painstakingly achieved.

The Prelude to Potential Relapse

The unforeseen loss of her job amid an economic downturn struck at the core of Emma's fears and insecurities. The sudden shift in her circumstances rekindled the embers of anxiety she thought she had subdued. Sleep became elusive, and her mind became a battleground for rumination and worry about the future. The sense of progress and stability she had fought so hard to achieve seemed to be slipping away, leaving her to confront the specter of relapse.

Mobilizing Coping Strategies

In the face of rising anxiety, Emma's first line of defense was to delve into the toolkit of coping strategies she had assembled during her journey of recovery. She recognized the critical importance of mindfulness meditation, a practice that had always served as an anchor, helping her remain present and grounded amidst life's tumultuous seas. By dedicating more time to meditation, Emma sought to cultivate an inner sanctuary of peace, away from the storm of external uncertainties.

Moreover, Emma revisited her commitment to physical wellness. Regular exercise, which had been sidelined by her distress, was reintroduced into her routine. The endorphin release from physical activity provided a natural counterbalance to anxiety, reaffirming the interconnectedness of physical and mental health.

Seeking and Offering Support

Understanding that isolation only amplifies anxiety, Emma activated her support network, reaching out to her therapist for an emergency session. This "booster" session served not only to reaffirm the coping strategies she had learned but also to explore new avenues for managing her current stressors. Emma's openness in sharing her struggles with friends and family further bolstered her support system, providing her with a sense of being understood and not alone in her journey.

Charting a New Course

In the crucible of this challenge, Emma discovered a reservoir of creativity and entrepreneurship she had not tapped into before. Channeling her passion for technology and art, she embarked on creating an online business that aligned with her hobbies and professional skills. This endeavor was not just a distraction but a transformational path that offered her a sense of purpose and direction amidst the chaos.

Reflection and Growth

Months later, as Emma reflects on this period of potential relapse, she views it not as a setback but as a pivotal phase in her journey of self-discovery and growth. The experience taught her the value of adaptability, the strength of her support network, and the power of resilience. Emma's story transcends her personal narrative, offering hope and inspiration to others navigating the complexities of anxiety management. It underscores the message that with awareness, support, and a willingness to adapt, it is possible to face potential relapses not as insurmountable obstacles but as opportunities for growth and renewal.

In summary, preventing relapse in anxiety management is an ongoing process that requires awareness, preparation, and support. By recognizing early warning signs, developing a personalized prevention plan, staying connected with support systems, and drawing inspiration from others' successes, individuals can maintain their progress and continue to live fulfilling lives, resilient in the face of challenges. This comprehensive approach to relapse prevention empowers individuals with the tools and confidence needed to keep anxiety at bay and embrace a journey of continuous personal growth and well-being.

Integrating Wellness Practices into Your Lifestyle

The journey toward mental well-being is continuous, and incorporating wellness practices into our daily routines greatly enhances this process. This comprehensive exploration delves into the multifaceted approach of embedding wellness into every day, aiming to provide a roadmap for individuals seeking sustained mental health benefits. Through practical strategies, an understanding of holistic wellness, and encouragement towards personal experimentation, this guide seeks to empower individuals to take proactive steps in their wellness journey.

Understanding the Impact of Routine Wellness Practices

Routine wellness practices serve as pillars for maintaining and enhancing mental health. They offer a stabilizing routine, a sense of control, and a proactive stance against anxiety. The daily repetition of these practices fosters a nurturing environment for mental well-being, enabling individuals to cultivate resilience against life's stressors and challenges.

Strategies for Incorporating Wellness into Daily Life

The integration of wellness practices into one's lifestyle demands intentionality and strategy. The goal is to transform these practices from occasional activities into non-negotiable elements of daily living.

- **Goal Setting for Success**: Begin by establishing specific, measurable, achievable, relevant, and time-bound (SMART) goals. For instance, rather than a vague intention to "exercise more," set a goal to "walk 30 minutes every weekday morning."

- **Harnessing the Power of Technology**: In our digital age, technology can be a powerful ally in managing wellness. Meditation apps offer guided sessions to fit any schedule, fitness trackers monitor physical activity and encourage movement, and nutritional apps help track eating habits. Setting digital reminders can also play a crucial role in forming new habits.

- **Creating a Wellness Calendar**: Schedule your wellness activities as you would any important appointment. This not only ensures time is set aside but also reinforces the importance of these activities in your daily routine.

Exploring the Dimensions of Holistic Wellness

Holistic wellness acknowledges that our well-being is not merely the absence of illness but a dynamic state of physical, emotional, and social health.

- **Physical Wellness through Lifestyle Choices**: Incorporate activities that nourish the body, like yoga or aerobics, and prioritize balanced nutrition and hydration. Experiment with different types of physical activities to find what energizes and relaxes you.

- **Cultivating Emotional Wellness**: Emotional wellness can be nurtured through practices like mindfulness meditation, expressive writing, and engaging in hobbies that bring joy and satisfaction. Regular practice of gratitude or keeping a gratitude journal can also enhance emotional well-being.

- **Fostering Social Wellness**: Strengthen social connections by actively seeking out and nurturing relationships that offer mutual support and understanding. Community involvement or group activities related to interests or hobbies can also enhance feelings of connectedness and belonging.

The Journey of Small Adjustments Leading to Significant Changes

Small, consistent changes in daily routines can lead to profound improvements in managing anxiety and enhancing overall well-being.

- **Integrating Mindfulness into Moments**: Incorporate brief mindfulness exercises into transitions throughout the day, such as deep breathing before meetings or mindful observation during breaks.

- **Nutritional Tweaks for Mood Enhancement**: Small dietary adjustments, such as incorporating omega-3-rich foods and reducing caffeine intake, can have noticeable effects on mood and energy levels.

Embracing Experimentation in the Wellness Journey

The path to wellness is highly individualized, emphasizing the importance of experimentation to discover what truly benefits you. Trial and error with different wellness practices, routines, and strategies are encouraged. Documenting experiences and reflections can be incredibly insightful, helping to tailor a wellness approach that fits your unique needs and lifestyle.

Integrating wellness practices into daily life is a transformative journey that extends beyond mere habit formation. It involves a deep commitment to nurturing one's physical, emotional, and social well-being, with the understanding that our health is our most precious asset. By setting realistic goals, leveraging technology, understanding the holistic nature of wellness, making incremental lifestyle adjustments, and adopting an experimental mindset, individuals can craft a life where wellness is not just practiced but lived This guide acts as a launching pad, motivating individuals to seize control of their wellness journey, discover what suits them best, and relish the significant advantages of living in harmony with their well-being.

CONCLUSION

CONTINUING YOUR JOURNEY

As we bring our journey through "Beyond Anxiety's Grasp" to a close, it's important to pause and reflect on the valuable insights and strategies we've uncovered together. This book has served as a roadmap, guiding you through the complexities of anxiety and offering tools to help you regain control and find peace. Let's take a moment to revisit the key takeaways, consider the continued path forward, and emphasize the importance of self-compassion and resilience.

Throughout these pages, we've explored the multifaceted nature of anxiety, highlighting that it's a condition that can be managed through a blend of therapy, medication, lifestyle changes, and mindfulness. The strategies presented, from cognitive-behavioral techniques to mindfulness meditation and the development of a personalized relapse prevention plan, are designed to empower you to navigate the challenges of anxiety effectively. Moreover, we've stressed the importance of holistic wellness, encouraging you to incorporate practices that nurture your mental, emotional, and physical well-being.

As you step beyond the confines of this book, remember that the journey to manage anxiety is ongoing. It's crucial to seek continued support, whether that's through professional therapy, support groups, or the embrace of loved ones. Keeping informed about new developments in anxiety management can provide additional tools and strategies to enhance your toolkit. Reflect on your progress regularly, celebrate your victories, and be open to adjusting your approach as your needs evolve.

Patience and kindness toward oneself are essential components of this journey. Progress may not consistently follow a straight path, and encountering setbacks is an inherent aspect of the journey. Treat yourself with the same compassion and understanding that you would offer a friend. Celebrate your achievements, no matter how small, and forgive yourself during moments of struggle. This attitude of self-compassion paves the way for sustained growth and well-being.

Remember, you are not defined by your anxiety. It is merely one aspect of your rich and complex identity. Within you lies strength, resilience, and the capacity for profound growth, qualities that far outweigh the challenges posed by anxiety. Let this knowledge be a source of hope and courage as you continue on your path.

In conclusion, "Beyond Anxiety's Grasp" is more than a guide—it's a testament to your determination to lead a life not overshadowed by anxiety, but illuminated by your dreams and aspirations. As this chapter ends and you look toward the future, take with you the knowledge, strategies, and sense of empowerment gained from these pages. The journey ahead may hold its uncertainties, but armed with these tools, you are well-equipped to navigate it with confidence and grace. Here's to moving forward, embracing growth, and living a life defined by your potential and passions.